CW00659600

A GARDEN IN SUSSEX

A GARDEN IN SUSSEX

PHOTOGRAPHS BY TESSA TRAEGER

FOREWORD BY STEWART GRIMSHAW

Published by The Cuckoo Press for John Sandoe (Books) Ltd
10 Blacklands Terrace, London SW3 2SR

A CIP catalogue reference for this book is available from the British Library

ISBN 10: 0 9542688 7 3   ISBN 13: 978 0 9542688 7 9

Cover and text design by Fenella Willis

Printed and bound in Italy by L.E.G.O. spa

For Simon
1930–2006

When we first moved to the country, we lived in a crenellated tower in Petworth Park. It was some time before we could tear ourselves away from 'Capability' Brown's mesmerising landscape; when we did, our forays through deep Sussex lanes revealed a wide valley little changed in centuries, thanks to the peculiarly English system of primogeniture and the good husbandry of a chain of great estates from Parham to Petworth, Cowdray, Goodwood and the Edward James estate at West Dean. Hilaire Belloc described this in *Hills and the Sea* (1906):

> The valley of the Rother is made of many parts. There is the chalk of the Southern Down-land, the belt of the loam beneath it; then the curious country of sand, full of dells and dark with pine woods; then the luxurious meadows which are open and full of cattle, colts and even sheep; then the woods. It is in a few miles a little England.

In time we contrived that our trips should pass an intriguing house whose Frenchified façade and overgrown garden resembled nothing so much as the magical abode for Perrault's Sleeping Beauty. Resorting to Pevsner and local libraries, we learned that it was still inhabited by two elderly ladies, a mother and daughter. Their forebears included Lord Robert Spencer, who had lived in a contented *ménage à trois* with Captain and Mrs Bouverie when the house was a celebrated Whig retreat; Charles James Fox – my only political hero, then MP for nearby Midhurst – was a frequent visitor.

On a Friday in November 1972, as we perused *Country Life* over breakfast, there in prime position we saw our dream house advertised:

> On a long lease from The National Trust, a delightful Grade II* listed Manor House comprising 4 Reception Rooms, Dining Room, Library, 22 Bedrooms, 2 Bathrooms – in need of considerable renovation.

As I ran to the nearest Knight, Frank & Rutley office, Simon ransacked his address book trying to contact anyone he had ever heard of within the Trust.

By dint of pleading and badgering we secured a visit on the following Monday.

Exhausted after viewing all two-and-twenty bedrooms, both bathrooms, pantry, gun room, boot room, flower room, housekeeper's sitting room and butler's quarters (with fireplace) – having strenuously ignored evidence of damp, both rising and falling – we coughed our way through clouds of assorted spores, declined to mention bugs and grubs as large as the newly introduced 1p coins, and agreed that the place was perfect for us.

Thus started a year of planning (principally for Simon) and 23 months of demolition and reparation which resulted, on time and within budget, in a more modest dwelling – only four guest bedrooms. Another benefit was the start of long and fruitful partnerships with the building contractors Taveners, a firm I use and cherish to this day, and Philip Jebb, a dream architect with whom we worked until his death in 1995. There was also the legacy of Philip's working drawings, so beautiful that they are possibly only surpassed by those of Charles Rennie Mackintosh.

For my part, on the basis of the slightest of acquaintanceships I somehow summoned up the nerve to approach the renowned garden designer Lanning Roper, whose early intervention prevented many major problems such as impaction and water-logging. He visited us at least twice a month, always on a Monday, and always when the rain and wind swept horizontally from the Downs. Such days came to be known as 'Lanning Days'.

We soaked up his sage advice: whence the prevailing winds; the breadth of paths – unless for effect, always wide enough for at least two people; where to have lunch outside (near the kitchen, of course); where to have drinks of an evening; how to plan a circuit to give purpose to our strolls, and a lesser route for the giddiest of our lady guests to enable them to teeter round on the level – a route, to boot, hard enough for the dizziest of stilettos.

And at last, with paths, terraces and steps installed we began work on the real gardening, starting with the broad vista from the Ionic pillared façade which had so charmed us, 'an impeccable formal approach' according to Ian Nairn's *Buildings of England* (1977). This is still framed by luxuriant flower borders: masses of white and blush roses, lilies, lavenders, alchemillas, white and blue cranesbills, irises, gypsophilas and astrantias, whose flowering season we extend year on year.

To the south of this vista a series of garden rooms was created, in a walled garden with an orangery designed by Philip in 1975. This, with its pool, occupies a highly formal room with related ports of call for vegetables, a decorative potager, herbs and cutting flowers. But the 'best' room is devoted to what was the real treasure of Woolbeding, a fountain with a young man standing on dolphins – attributed to Cellini, later Rustici and then (downgraded still further) Benedetto da Rovezzano. It was stolen and, astonishingly, recovered in Australia, and has been replaced by a cast copy. The original is now in the V&A.

Working with Lanning, as I did from 1974 until 1977, was a real joy. Until his death in 1983 he kept an eye on things as they developed, encouraging or gently criticising. It was very pleasing to read in his biography by Jane Brown (1987) that the work we did brought him 'a great deal of pleasure'.

Throughout the 1980s we consolidated this early groundwork, altering and adding a few features, always mindful of Lanning's maxim that we must be able comfortably to maintain what we had created before moving on to a new enterprise. We created a lake in marshy land across the river and planned to stock it with wild fowl, an ambition that remains unfulfilled after a run-in with a pair of black swans in the back of a Jeep on the M1.

We had fallen heir to many remarkable trees: two spreading Oriental planes, layering as they snaked outwards, linked by a hornbeam tunnel; an immense black walnut in front of the stables whose citrus-smelling fruits scent the air in autumn; three magisterial cedars; and, best of all, a tulip tree, cited as the largest in Europe in Elwes & Henry 1907.

A victim of the storm in October 1987, the latter fell diagonally across the croquet lawn, defying the laws of physics in its trajectory and missing the house by inches. The simple monument we erected to this old friend was designed by Philip Jebb, and was his last commission for us before his death. During our association Philip had transformed my doodles into a series of structures, although quite how a charming arbor became known to my gardeners as 'the bus shelter' or the reminder of the tulip tree became a 'temple', I know not. And the house itself, in a fit of self-aggrandisement, mysteriously emerged as Grade I listed, which has proved to be a bother and a bore ever since.

If our activities with Lanning and Philip had been a pleasure and an education, then our next collaboration proved to be a hoot. Working with Isabel and Julian Bannerman on the biggest assignment so far, we envisaged a woodland walk at the furthest end of the garden, beyond the paddock and cricket field. After a year in the planning and two in the execution – the Bannerman's limitless enthusiasm tempered by Simon's natural restraint – the result was a pleasure ground with a ruined abbey, hermit's hut, Chinese bridge, rustic walk, grotto with river god, Gothic summer house, waterfall, rills, stumpery and bubbling source, roughly in that sequence. This partnership avoided the pitfalls of excess, producing something less like a Disney attraction, which it might so easily have become, and more in keeping with our gentler environs. As Simon's health deteriorated, he loved working with these ebullient, talented people, and I shall forever be grateful to them.

It seemed to be time for us to take stock of what we had done and, after seeing her exhibition at the National Portrait Gallery, I invited Tessa Traeger to photograph our efforts. Over a two-year period, she responded with great sensitivity to the garden's unique rhythms and routines, often rising before dawn to capture effects she anticipated, as well as seizing chance moments throughout the day in a way which began to change my habits. Never previously an early riser, I now often get up in the dark and take advantage of an hour or more of the garden before breakfast. Tessa finished the project in August 2006, having become a true friend in the process.

Before he died that September, Simon saw all of these photographs, not bound in a book but scattered, hundreds of them, over a large table in Tessa's studio.

He thought they were beautiful.

STEWART GRIMSHAW

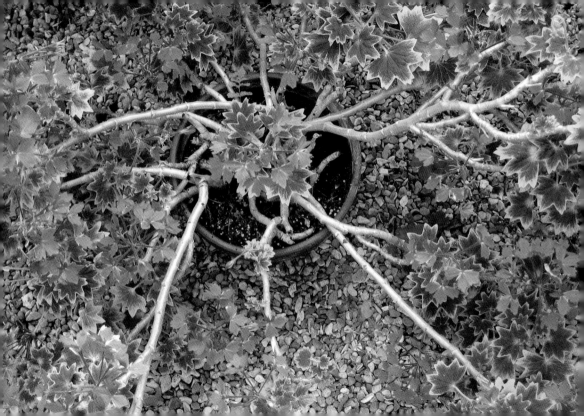

For more information about these images, please visit
www.johnsandoe.com/our_publications.htm